Stars in the Shadows

THE NEGRO LEAGUE ALL-STAR GAME OF 1934

by Charles R. Smith Jr.   *illustrated by* Frank Morrison

Atheneum Books for Young Readers
NEW YORK • LONDON • TORONTO • SYDNEY • NEW DELHI

ATHENEUM BOOKS FOR YOUNG READERS
An imprint of Simon & Schuster Children's Publishing Division
1230 Avenue of the Americas, New York, New York 10020
Text copyright © 2012 by Charles R. Smith Jr.
Illustrations copyright © 2012 by Frank Morrison
ATHENEUM BOOKS FOR YOUNG READERS is a registered trademark
of Simon & Schuster, Inc.
For information about special discounts for bulk purchases,
please contact Simon & Schuster Special Sales at 1-866-506-1949
or business@simonandschuster.com.
The Simon & Schuster Speakers Bureau can bring authors to your
live event. For more information or to book an event, contact the
Simon & Schuster Speakers Bureau at 1-866-248-3049 or visit our
website at www.simonspeakers.com.
Book design by Lauren Rille
The text for this book is set in Candida.
The illustrations for this book are rendered in graphite.
Manufactured in the United States of America
1211 FFG
First Edition
10 9 8 7 6 5 4 3 2 1
CIP data for this book is available from the Library of Congress.
ISBN 978-0-689-86638-8
ISBN 978-1-4424-5076-9 (eBook)

To Adrian and Sebastian,

who will never have to play in the shadows,

thanks to all those who did

—C. R. S. Jr.

To my new shortstop, Tiffani

—F. M.

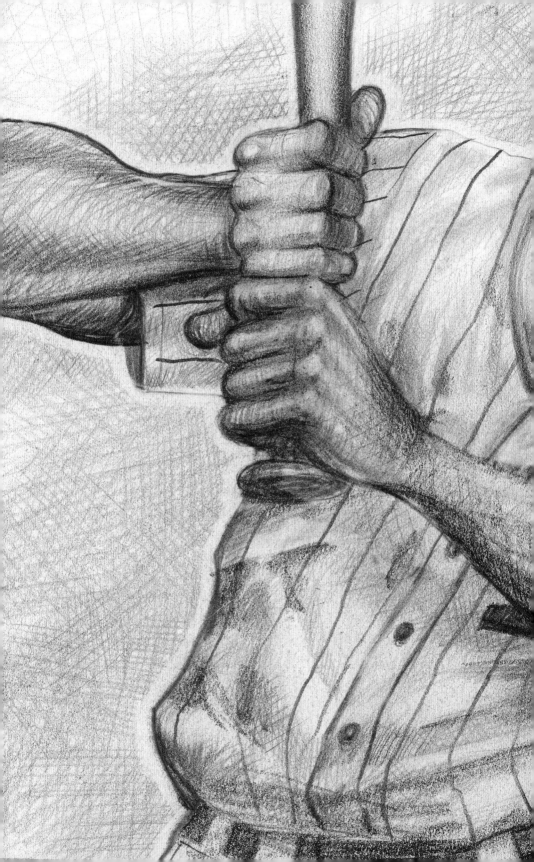

Welcome to **Chicago**, welcome all!
   It's a beautiful day to play baseball.
Bright sun with not one single cloud in the sky,
a blue-curtain backdrop to watch baseballs fly.
Hello, everybody, to you from me,
Lester Roberts, on your radio on WNLB,
bringing you the play-by-play in a creative way
of the second annual Negro League East-West game
   today.
Last year's game was fun-filled with eighteen runs,
including a cannon shot that came from
the bat of Mule Suttles, who swung his barrel chest
and arms to launch a four-bag express
into center-field stands, sending slug-happy fans
into a frenzy, making sepia hands
clap and cheer and throw hats into the air,

a heart-stopping moment for all who were there.
But that was last year—now it's on to
the Negro League East-West Classic number two,
featuring players voted in by you,
the fans who follow this game through and through.
But before our game starts and before we do
    anything,
first we will hear "Lift Every Voice and Sing,"
the Negro National Anthem, sung by the Jubilee
Singers, representing our wonderful Windy City.
What better way to start this glorious day,
so let's listen in as they take it away.

Lift every voice and sing
Till earth and heaven ring,
Ring with the harmonies of Liberty;
Let our rejoicing rise
High as the listening skies,
Let it resound loud as the rolling sea.
Sing a song full of the faith that the dark
*   past has taught us,*
Sing a song full of the hope that the
*   present has brought us;*
Facing the rising sun of our new day begun,
Let us march on till victory is won.

Thank you, performers, and again welcome all.

Enjoy the show, folks,

now let's
PLAY
BALL!

Cool Papa Bell

Slim Jones

Josh Gibson

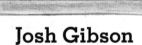

Dick Lundy

Vic Harris

Oscar Charleston

Jud Wilson

EAST

Chester Williams

Jimmie Crutchfield

Willie Wells

Alex Radcliffe

WEST

Mule Suttles

Ted Trent

Turkey Stearnes

Red Parnell

Sammy
Hughes

Sam
Bankhead

Larry Brown

Now we begin with introductions for
each team's starting nine, determined by your
votes in Negro newspapers in various cities,
giving you, the fans, power, not a secret committee.
We start with the East, who last year suffered defeat,
an outcome I'm sure they don't want to repeat.
In center field, leading off and doing it well,
the speed demon known as Cool Papa Bell.
Playing right field, Jimmie Crutchfield,
and fielding balls at base number one,
the legendary all-star Oscar Charleston.
On third base, Jud Wilson,
then the slugger Josh Gibson,
who will crouch at home plate in the catcher's
    position.
In left field, Vic Harris,
followed by Dick Lundy,
the shortstop who always throws on the money.
At second, Chester Williams, and setting the tone
from atop the mound, the pitcher, Slim Jones.
Now to the West I direct your ears,
the All-Star Game's first victors last year.
Leading off for his team like his East counterpart, Bell,
the Shakespeare of Shortstops, Willie "the Devil"
    Wells.

At third, Alex Radcliffe,

and then Turkey Stearnes,

who will trot through center field with feathered
    speed to burn.

Next up is Mule Suttles, working first base,

and then Red Parnell, who takes his place

in left field, and he will be followed by

Sam Bankhead, the fielder in right shagging flies.

Larry Brown will catch,

followed by Sammy Hughes, the crack

infielder who covers the keystone sack.

Last but not least on the hill for the West,

Ted Trent toes the slab in this classic contest.

The West team parades out onto the field,

and here we go, folks, so keep your ears peeled.

But first here's a word from one of our sponsors who

helped bring this radio broadcast to you.

Run out of sugar?
Well, we got that.
Need more butter?
Well, we got that.
Need beans?
Need rice?

Well, we also got that.
We got all that and more
at Arrow's Market.
Come visit Arrow's
and be sure you don't miss
the best prices around
on items like this:

a gallon of milk for 22 cents,
a pound of bacon for 29 cents,
and a 10-pound sack of potatoes
for 23 cents.
So when your groceries are gone,
just come on down
to Arrow's Market
on the South Side of town.

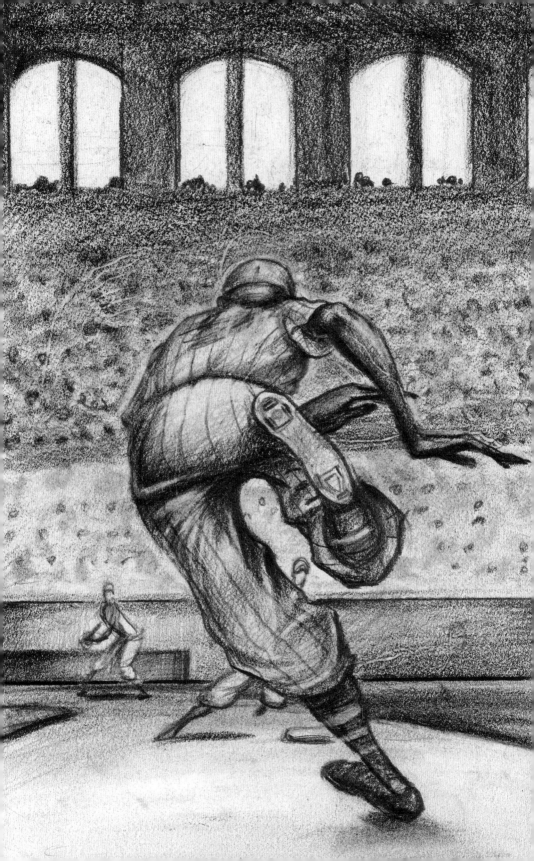

Top of the 1st Inning

Due Up:

Cool Papa Bell, CF (Pittsburgh Crawfords)
Jimmie Crutchfield, RF (Pitt. Crawfords)
Oscar Charleston, 1B (Pitt. Crawfords)

Leading off for the East, the speedster fans know
as Cool Papa Bell has been known to go
faster than ANY player in the game,
Negro or white, and he's made a name
for himself by creating legends and myth
surrounding his speed, but he now gets a whiff
of Ted Trent, whose fastball notches strike two
on the Tan Cheetah, who scratches each shoe
into the dirt, itching to run.
Now Trent flings a pitch off the plate for ball one.
Known to turn singles into quick doubles,
Cool Papa on base for an infield spells trouble,
so the players move closer as Trent lets fly
a southbound freight train that Bell swats high

high into right,

but Sam Bankhead gives chase and ends the ball's
  flight.

Out number one and a good thing too

because Cool Papa was speeding past base number
  two

and pulling up standing into base number three,

amazing all fans with his lightning-like ability.

As Bell gallops off, up comes Jimmie

Crutchfield, the right fielder, born in Missouri.

Standing just five feet seven inches tall,

folks, this man's talent is anything but small.

Playing for the mighty Crawfords in Pittsburgh,

his spot on this team is truly deserved.

His feet are fleet, his bat is swift,

and his slingshot of an arm is powered by grit.

Trent seems more focused on what he has to do

as Crutchfield swings late on a fastball—

Strike 2.

The count stands even at two balls and two strikes

as Trent eyeballs his catcher for a sign that he likes.

He shakes, then nods his head to agree,

winds up and releases a changeup—

STRIKE 3.

Crutchfield goes down as Trent racks up a K,

the first of this East-West Classic today.

The pitcher the fans know as High Pockets stands

tall on the mound, displaying the command

that has made him one of the best,

and why he's the first on the hill for the West.

But now comes a test as fans rise from their seats,

because Oscar Charleston has this crowd on its feet.

Ten plus nine years in this game,

he packs a mean punch in his wide-bodied frame.

With the speed of Ty Cobb and the power of Babe
   Ruth,

Oscar Charleston, folks, is indeed the truth.

His speed may have slowed and perhaps his bat, too,

but there is still plenty this living legend can do.

A FAN IN THE STANDS

SECTION 320, CLUB LEVEL, FIRST BASE SIDE

"Well, well, well. Whaddya say there? If it ain't the legendary Oscar Charleston comin' up to bat. Yes sir, I sure been waitin' to see you play. I done seen all the great colored players, starting with Fleet Walker and Bud

Fowler. Yes sir, the first couple of colored players ever, and I seen 'em! They said you could really spin your wheels back in the day, running down those fly balls in center field with speed to burn and flair to spare. I see they got you playing first base now. I guess your wheels got a little rusty with age, huh? Is it true you used to show off that glove of yours by catching the ball with your back to the crowd and that sometimes you did a flip before you caught it? I'll bet a plate of sweet yams and greens down at Sweet Amelia's that you did. And I'm sure that was a sight to see, yes sir. My cousin down south in Sunflower, Mississipp', told me that one time you put a lickin' on a ball so hard you sent it a country mile and made that pitcher cry. Ain't that something? He also told me about that hot temper of yours. Yeah, I heard about them scuffles you got into with your opponents and teammates, and that just lets me know you got the fire. Yes sir, Oscar, you got the fire in you. As long as you got a field to play ball on, you and all the other Negro Leaguers will always have a fan in me. I don't care what anybody say, you all are equally as good as them fellas in the white major leagues. I seen a lot in my life, but I can't wait to see what you can do. So let's go, Oscar . . . SHOW ME SOME OF THAT FIRE!"

The count stands full as Trent lets fly
a changeup that Charleston smacks into the sky,
deep into left field, where Red Parnell awaits.
That ball is gonna carry, so Parnell gives chase
and makes a great catch for out number three,
making a difficult play look so easy.

Bottom of the 1st Inning
Due Up:
Willie Wells, SS (Chicago American Giants)
Alex Radcliffe, 3B (Chi. Amer. Giants)
Turkey Stearnes, CF (Chi. Amer. Giants)

We now have the East team taking the field,
with hard-throwing southpaw Slim Jones on the hill.

A tall drink of water standing six foot six,
this long and lean lefty will test the West's sticks
with a fastball that sizzles smoke over the plate.
Slim's arm versus the bats of the West should be
　　great!
First up to bat, a young fella you all know,
Willie Wells, the shortstop, known as El Diablo.
The Devil weighs in at a buck sixty-six
and stands sixty-nine inches, but moves with cat-
　　quick
reflexes to snag anything hit
in his direction—and more than just that,
this sure-handed short fielder has pop in his bat,
something these fans might not get to see
as the umpire calls ball number three.
With three balls and one strike, Slim falls behind
to Wells in the count and can't seem to find
the strike zone as he throws all over the place,
and ball number four puts the Devil on base.
If Slim hopes to last long in this game today,
he needs to elevate his level of play,
and a leadoff walk is not a good way
to start off the game; he needs a whiff—
let's see what he can do with Alex Radcliffe,
the sturdy third baseman who bats from the right.

Slim winds up and sends a strike high and tight.
Radcliffe steps out of the box to gather his swing,
then steps back in to see Slim sling
another fastball for strike number two.
Radcliffe swung swift, but folks, that ball blew
right by him as Slim made him chase
a chest-high heater out over the plate.
Wells waits on first, the result of a walk.
Slim breaks his windup and commits a balk,
so Wells will take second, leaving first base free,
but Slim exhales and hurls Radcliffe strike three.
The next out, folks, will not be easy,
because next up to bat is the hard-hitting Turkey—
Stearnes, that is, who calls center field
his home, and boy, can he hit, throw, and steal.
As a matter of fact, he is the only player to
win the quadruple crown and that was just two
years ago, when he led the Negro Southern League
in doubles, triples, homers, and stolen bases,
a feat never done in the league of white faces,
and something only done by Oscar the Great.
But let me direct your ears back to home plate,
where Josh Gibson, the catcher, has just thrown a
    shot
to Wilson at third, and his strong arm caught

Wells trying to steal as Josh closed the deal
on out number two for Slim on the hill.
But now back to Turkey, where Slim turns his vision
and sends in strike two on the corner with precision.
Ahead in the count with one ball and two strikes,
Slim kicks up his leg, then sends down the pipe

a pitch that pulls Turkey into a swing,
deceiving the bird as Slim pulls the string
on a changeup that uses the same delivery
as his blazing fastball to earn strike number three.
The first inning, folks, is now in the books
as Slim brought the heat and Turkey got cooked.

Top of the 2nd Inning

Due Up:

Jud Wilson, 3B (Philadelphia Stars)

Josh Gibson, C (Pitt. Crawfords)

Vic Harris, LF (Pitt. Crawfords)

We start the second with third baseman Jud Wilson
on first from a walk, and at the plate is Gibson,
Josh—"Oh my gosh!"—the one that they call
the Brown Bambino because he swats the ball
out of stadiums with Herculean glory,
each moon shot creating another mythical story.

A FAN IN THE STANDS

SECTION 128, LOWER DECK RESERVED,
FIRST BASE SIDE OVER DUGOUT

"Josh Gibson is coming up to bat?
Is that the Josh Gibson y'all been telling
me about?

The Josh Gibson who plays for the Crawfords back home in Pittsburgh?

The same Josh Gibson who hit a ball so hard and so high in a game that it disappeared and then dropped out of the sky the next day?

Is that the Josh Gibson who swatted a ball out of the park with one hand like he was shooing away a fly?

The same Josh Gibson who hits balls so hard he punches holes in center-field bleachers?

Is that really the Josh Gibson that hit seventy-five home runs in ONE year?

The same Josh Gibson you said hit a ball OUT of Yankee Stadium?

Out like over-the-highest-seat-and-bouncing-onto-the-street out of the park?

And didn't you say he is the only player to ever do that?

Is that the same Josh Gibson everybody

calls the Brown Bambino? The black Babe Ruth?

Because if all of that is true, then it sounds to me like they should call Babe Ruth 'the white Josh Gibson.'"

The pitcher, Ted Trent, has fallen behind
in the count; he delivers . . . and Gibson sends a line
drive hit between first and second base.
Wilson will scoot to second and Gibson takes his
    place
on first as the fans erupt in the stands
cheering the black Babe Ruth with wild clapping
    hands.
In the box now is left fielder Vic
Harris, who swings a mean left-handed stick.
With the count even at two and two,
Trent nods, then lifts and plants his left shoe
into the dirt, putting all he's got
into his pitch, but Vic sends a hot
shot over to third, where Radcliffe awaits,
catching out number one—then he steps on third
    base
for out number two, stopping Jud Wilson

from scoring, leaving the slugger Josh Gibson
on second base with a fine double play,
as the West team stands just one out away
from ending the inning—but out number three
will be earned as shortstop/manager Dick Lundy
stands at the plate looking to drive in
the first run of the day, his teammate Josh Gibson.
Trent is ahead with one ball and two
strikes on Lundy, the switch-hitter who
swings on strike three, as Trent sits him down
by twisting a curve like a top from the mound.
Trent quiets the thunder of these mighty East sticks
by reaching into his bag of crafty pitch tricks,
notching another goose egg on the board,
leaving Gibson stranded in an effort to score.

If your tongue has a taste
for food from the South,
Sweet Amelia's Soul Cuisine
has treats for your mouth.
Roast beef,
fresh catfish,
or country ham,
Sweet Amelia's Soul Cuisine
comes fresh from her hand.
She's got greens,
macaroni,
and yams,
and makes sweet potato pie
like nobody can.
Black-eyed peas
and cornbread, too,
Sweet Amelia's Soul Cuisine
has something for you.
So come on down
and have a taste
'cause Sweet Amelia's Soul Cuisine
will put a smile on your face.

SWEET AMELIA'S SOUL CUISINE

Bottom of the 2nd Inning

Due Up:
Mule Suttles, 1B (Chi. Amer. Giants)
Red Parnell, LF (Nashville Elite Giants)
Sam Bankhead, RF (Nash. E. Giants)

Welcome back, folks. The West has come alive
with two quick hits from batters four and five.
Mule Suttles kicked a single up the first base line;
then Red Parnell punched a double behind
Oscar Charleston at first, making Jimmie Crutchfield
    give chase,
but he made a great throw to hold Red on second
    base.
Right fielder Sam Bankhead next went down
on swinging strikes, which brings us to Larry Brown.
With two on and one out, Brown of the West
will not give the hard-throwing Slim Jones a rest.
He circles his bat in the right batter's box,
and the pitch comes to Brown, who swings hard and
    socks
a chopper to Lundy, the diving shortstop,
who backhands the ball on a short hop.
Suttles charges from third to home plate
to score, but Lundy leaps up to make

a hard throw home, saving a run,
meaning this rally, folks, could be done.
But up next is second baseman Sammy Hughes,
whose bat right now his team could sure use
to score Red Parnell standing on second base,
as Slim Jones, the pitcher, wipes sweat from his face,
tugs on his cap, then raises his mitt,
winds up, and releases a fastball Hughes hits
over to first, where Oscar Charleston grabs
the hard grounder, then steps on the first bag
for out number three, sitting the West down,
allowing no runs for Slim on the mound.

Top of the 3rd Inning
Due Up:
Chester Williams, 2B (Pitt. Crawfords)
Slim Jones, P (Philadelphia Stars)
Cool Papa Bell

We begin the third with Ted Trent behind
in the count to Chester Williams, the fine
second baseman who swings on Trent's 3-1 pitch.
Williams connects with a hard chopper hit
to the left middle infield and kicks up a cloud
of dust as Wells, the shortstop, wows the crowd
with a lunging backhand grab that stops
the ball; then he spins on his knees and hops
up to toss the ball to bag one,
nailing Williams on a play only Wells could have
    done.
Wow, that was Willie "the Devil" in action,
showcasing his skill for your satisfaction.

A FAN IN THE STANDS

"Heckuva grab there, Willie! But then I've learned to expect that from you. Willie 'the Devil' Wells. The Shakespeare of Shortstops. You sure do have some colorful nicknames, I tell you what. I done scouted many players over the years and all I can say, Willie, is that you got it. You got *it*. A great mitt. You got some pop in that bat *and* you can hit for average. Yeah, your arm ain't that strong, but man oh man, can you get to those balls quick. I seen you play in Cuba with some of the white major leaguers and Cubans, and I tell you what, you stood out like a fox in a henhouse. The fans was all chanting 'El Di-ablo, El Di-ablo, El Di-ablo,' and I knew they was talkin' about you because you are some kind of devil with that mitt of yours. The one with the hole in the middle; I heard it made your job on the field easier. Go figure! There was no missing you on the field, I tell you what. I seen you play deep at short and make catches that center fielders would have to run in for. But not you. All that speed and range mixed with them baseball smarts in your head make you one of the best I've ever seen. Not just Negro. Not just white. One of the best, period. I can think of at least ten players right now in the bigs that couldn't carry your mitt, Willie. If you wasn't a Negro, I would sign you up for my team, the White Sox, in a jackrabbit's heartbeat. Shucks, if it was up to me, I'd have just about the whole lot of you on the field here today, playing in the bigs. I don't care about the owners and their baloney 'gentlemen's agreement' to keep you boys out of the league. You boys can play and you should be showing your skills in the big show."

The East will now sit after outs two and three were made by Slim Jones and Cool Papa, respectively.

Slim sat down on strikes, and Cool Papa sent
a shot straight to third that instantly went
into the mitt of Radcliffe, who played
in much closer and easily made
a great catch that sat the East team back
     down,
sending Slim Jones of the West back up to
     the mound.

Bottom of the 3rd Inning
Due Up:
Ted Trent, P (Chi. Amer. Giants)
Willie Wells
Alex Radcliffe

Back to the game I take you again,
with two outs already from the pitching of Slim.
Three strikes sent Ted Trent quick
but Willie "the Devil" Wells swung his stick
and connected on a ball that was scooped up by
shortstop Dick Lundy, who then let fly
a hard throw to first for out number two,
which brings us to Radcliffe, the third baseman, who

now stands in the box waiting to see
what Slim will throw next when the count stands at
    three
balls and one strike as Slim begins his delivery
and releases a pitch that Radcliffe sees well
as he smacks a line drive, sending Cool Papa Bell
back in center field as the ball rises high,
but the fleet feet of Bell help him track down the fly.
That was out number three, but folks, we've got
    more
to come as we head to the top of inning four.

Is your wardrobe dull
with no style or pizzazz?
Then what you need
is A Dash of Class.
We got suits,
we got pants,
we got shirts
and shoes.
And yes, we have hats
at A Dash of Class too.
We got bowlers and fedoras
with brims that snap

in many different sizes,
and we also have caps.
We got suspenders
and socks
and belts
and ties
and overcoats, too,
for when it's cold outside.
So run—don't walk—
to A Dash of Class
on the South Side when you
want style and pizzazz.

Top of the 4th Inning

Due Up:
Jimmie Crutchfield
Oscar Charleston
Jud Wilson

We begin the fourth inning with a new face,
Chet Brewer, the pitcher who will replace
Ted Trent of the West, and folks, you will see
that this six-foot-four pitcher who plays for the K. C.
Monarchs can hurl the apple with zip
and tie up a batter with a curveball that dips
from the nose to the toes, creating a combination
that surely will bring the East team frustration.
Some of you may have heard Chet Brewer's name
mentioned before in connection with a game
that took place just four short years ago
when he battled the great pitcher Smokey Joe.

Starting in the seventh, Chet put on a show,
striking out with ease ten batters in a row.
From inning number one to number twelve at the
    end,
Chet gave up four hits and earned his team the win.
But that was back then—now let's get back to
the man on the hill, Chet Brewer, who
during my story earned outs one, two, and three
on Crutchfield, Charleston, and Wilson quickly.

Bottom of the 4th Inning

Due Up:
Turkey Stearnes
Mule Suttles
Red Parnell

On the hill for the East we have a new man,
Harry Kincannon, better known as Tin Can.
Working fast, he quickly earns
out number one on Turkey Stearnes
by coaxing his bat to launch a pop
fly that was caught by Lundy, the shortstop.
Next up is Mule Suttles, the righty with might

who loads up and swings strong through a strike,
bringing the count to two balls and one
strike as Tin Can squints from the sun,
tugs on his sleeves, and scratches his cleats
on the slab while Suttles digs in his feet.
The pitch is released and Suttles drives
a high fly to left that Vic Harris dives
for, but he misses the ball as it kisses
the grass, then rolls beyond his mitt.
Suttles is chugging, chug-chugging toward third
on a stand-up triple that, folks, could be heard
throughout the park to the top of the seats
as the fans here are up and cheering on their feet.
The West will now threaten and look to get ahead
on a hit to score Suttles from the next batter, Red
Parnell, the left fielder, who approaches the box
    slow,
surveying to see where his hit should go.
Harry on the hill hurls a strike above the knees,
takes the ball back, appearing at ease,
then winds up a changeup that escapes and creeps
toward Red, who connects on a ball that leaps
off his bat and into the sky,
drifting toward right, where it continues to fly
toward Jimmie Crutchfield, who ensnares the ball

in his mitt, then plants and unloads all
of that slingshot arm into a throw that chases
Mule Suttles, who waits for the catch, then races
from third base to home, looking to score the first
  run—
but Gibson blocks the plate, tags him OUT, and he's
  done!
A great double play for outs two and three,
from the glove and the arm of right fielder Jimmie
Crutchfield, whose play has every one of these fans
voicing their joy with thunderous hands.

A FAN IN THE STANDS
SECTION 113, LOWER DECK
RESERVED, FIRST BASE LINE

"Great play, Crutch! They don't know
your arm like I know your arm, because they
don't know about Jimmie C. like I know
about Jimmie C. I been watching you for a
long time now, so I know what you can do.
My daddy used to take me to watch you
play when he finished his work in the coal
mines in Moberly, Missouri. I remember

watching you run barefoot around the bases and chasing down fly balls like a bug in the outfield. I always liked you, Crutch, 'cause even though you was small, you played like somebody ten times bigger. My daddy used to say to me: 'Boy, don't you ever let your small size hold you back. You see Crutch out there playing and he ain't no bigger than a termite. Size don't matter. What matters is heart!' And I know you got a big ol' heart in that little body of yours, Jimmie. That's why I want to be just like you when I grow up. I may be small, but I got heart. Just like you, Jimmie Crutch, the Mite from Moberly."

Top of the 5th Inning

Due Up:
Josh Gibson
Vic Harris
Dick Lundy, SS (Newark Dodgers)

Josh Gibson approaches the box with ambition,
with fire in his eyes like a man on a mission,
but Brewer on the hill doesn't blink or show fear
at the sight of the slugger who inspires great cheer.
The pitcher kicks up his leg and then lets fly
strike one down the pipe, a fastball letter-high.
Brewer digs back in and so does Gibson,
giving the hurler his undivided attention.
The next pitch is low, bringing ball one, so
the count stands even as the crowd exhales slow,
waiting, anticipating to see what's next
and Brewer sends a strike past Gibson's chest.

One ball and two strikes have put Gibson behind
the cool, crafty pitcher, who begins his windup motion and propels a fastball from way back,
but Josh gets on track and wallops a smack
that sends the ball deep, deep into the pasture
of center field, where Turkey Stearnes is trotting
    faster
and faster and faster, going way back
as the hard-hit ball hurtles toward the warning track.
Turkey picks up his quick-feathered trot,
reaches the fence, leaps . . . and IT'S CAUGHT
by the high-flying fowl who steals away
a homer from Gibson on a GREAT play!

A FAN IN THE STANDS
SECTION 163, LEFT FIELD BLEACHERS
"Gobble gobble! Gobble that ball up, Turkey! I can't believe you just robbed Josh Gibson of a four-bagger right in front of my very own eyes! This Pullman porter from Nashville has finally seen the Thanksgiving bird in action. And boy how-dee, was that

some kind of action! Speakin' of Nashville, one of my buddies told me that you was from Nashville too. How 'bout them apples? Me from Nashville, watching you, Turkey Stearnes, from Nashville too. Imagine that? I been to plenty of Negro League games, from Loozyana to Alabama and New York City to Kansas City, and I heard about you, Turkey, oh yeah, I heard all about you, Turkey Stearnes. But I never seen you play, and I tell you what, Turkey, you sure got a funny way of chasing down them balls in the outfield. Your head gets to bobbing, your arms get to flapping, and your legs get to chopping . . . no wonder they call you Turkey!"

Well, folks, outs two and three came quickly
as Vic Harris struck out and shortstop Dick Lundy
hit a comebacker to an alert Chet
Brewer, who made a great grab to get
out number three for the hard-working West.

Bottom of the 5th Inning

Due Up:

Sam Bankhead

Larry Brown, C (Chi. Amer. Giants)

Sammy Hughes, 2B (Nash. E. Giants)

We begin the bottom of the fifth, moving swift.
Tin Can on the hill gave up one hit
to Sam Bankhead, who singled past third to get on,
but an attempt to steal second was stopped by Josh
    Gibson.
The hard throw from Josh sat Bankhead down,
allowing Tin Can to focus on Larry Brown.
Brown steps out of the box, then slowly back in
and directs his eyes to Tin Can, who begins
his windup and uncoils a tightly wound whip
that cracks toward Brown, who slaps a chip
shot over the head of Oscar Charleston toward right,
earning a single to this crowd's delight.
Tin Can shakes it off by turning his eyes
to the next batter and sending a fastball that flies
right past the letters on Sammy Hughes's chest,
now heaving, so he will take a brief moment's rest
by kicking his cleats before digging back in.

Hughes connects on a pitch that is caught by
    Charleston,
making out number two with one out left,
bringing up the number nine hitter, Chet
Brewer, the pitcher, who stares at strike one
as Brown bounces on first, hoping to run.
Here comes pitch two, and Chet softly connects
on a slow roller to second that Chester Williams gets
and throws to Charleston for out number three,
effectively ending the West's rally.
The West had two chances at scoring a run,
but Tin Can squeaked by and the inning is now
    done.

Top of the 6th Inning
Due Up:
Chester Williams
Tin Can Kincannon, P (Pitt. Crawfords)
Cool Papa Bell

Back to the action I now return you,
with one out on the East and one player who
stands at first base, Chester Williams, who hit
a single that jumped past Mule Suttles's mitt.
The burly first baseman almost made a great
catch, but he missed, so we turn to the plate
to see the Tan Cheetah, Cool Papa Bell,
poke a line drive to left fielder Parnell.
Cool Papa takes off, looking to get
to first base and more, but Parnell won't let
that happen as he makes the catch easily,
making two outs and bringing up Jimmie

Crutchfield, the right fielder who's played splendidly.
No hits for Crutch, but a great double play
provided one of the best moments today.
Four straight balls will put Jimmie on base
and paint a frustrated look on Chet's face.
With two outs gone but two men on,
the East is threatening to score the first run,
and what better player for this situation
than Oscar the Great for a home-run demonstration.
Today he's come close but hasn't connected
the bat and the ball like some folks expected.
Brewer winds up and sends home strike two,
making Charleston swing through
a curveball that dipped from his chest to his shoe.
That strike and three balls make the count full,
so Charleston steps out, snorting like a bull
as Brewer looks in to his catcher, Brown,
and gives Oscar the gas from high on the mound.
Charleston swings and uncorks a pop
that line-drives to Willie Wells, the shortstop,
who makes the tag on Williams, closing the door
on the East team's chance to notch the first score.

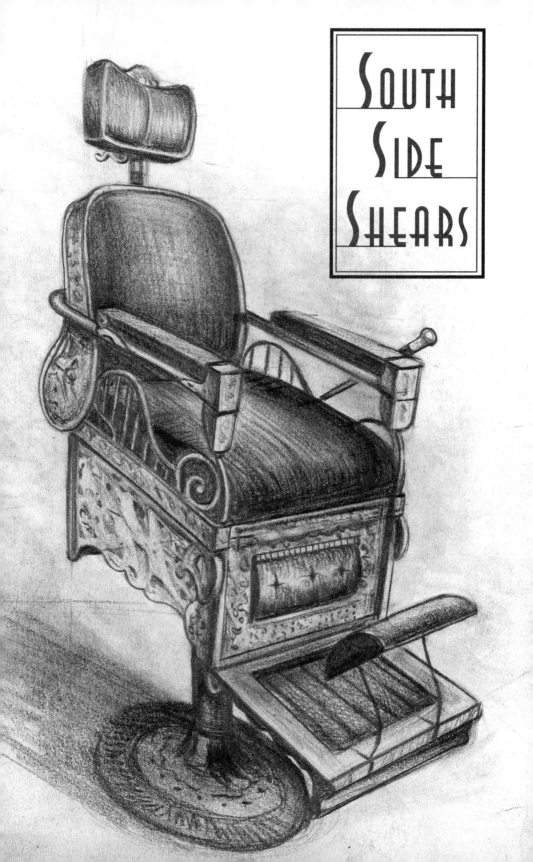

SOUTH
SIDE
SHEARS

Got too much on top
and you need a chop?
Is your hair so long
you can't see your ears?
Then come to Smitty's
South Side Shears.
Whether your 'do is too tall
or even itty-bitty,
stroll to the South Side . . .
and look up Smitty!

Bottom of the 6th Inning

Due Up:
Willie Wells
Alex Radcliffe
Turkey Stearnes

The West is back up and we begin with Willie
Wells, the shortstop, who just took ball three.
Tin Can on the hill has thrown only one strike,
so Willie can wait for a pitch that he likes.
The next pitch looks good, so Wells swings and
　　connects
on a sinker that drops and rolls into left.
Vic Harris fields the ball after giving chase,
but Wells earns a double sliding into second base.
Manager Dick Lundy approaches the hill,
pats Tin Can on the back, and takes back the pill.
And look who's coming out to replace
Tin Can on the hill, a legendary face:
the great Satchel Paige—some call him the best—
yes, Satchel Paige, folks, will try to shut down the
　　West.

FANS IN THE STANDS

SMITTY'S SOUTH SIDE SHEARS

Customer #1: "It's over for the West now, fellas, 'cause Satchel the Great is coming into the game. Best pitcher in history, that Satchel is!"

Barber #1: "Oh, here we go. Satchel Paige! Satchel Paige! Satchel Paige! Everybody always got somethin' to say about Satchel Paige. Satchel this, Satchel that. 'He's so good . . . he's so great . . . blah, blah, blah.' I hear you talkin', but you ain't sayin' nuthin'. Yeah, Satchel's good; some would say great. But I can name a handful of other pitchers that would pitch Satchel under the mound.

I'll give you one name right now: Bullet Joe Rogan. Boom! What you know about that, youngblood?"

Barber #2: "Oh, come on now, Ray, you know that young buck ain't ready for the Bullet.

He was probably still scraping his knees on his mama's floor when Joe was puttin' it to 'em on the hill."

Customer #2: "Bullet Joe, who's that? I think my daddy may have said somethin' about him, but who is he?"

Barber #1: "Who was Bullet Joe? In a pecan nutshell, Bullet Joe was the only pitcher who could not only strike you out from the hill but whack the ball out of the park from the plate. That's right. Most pitchers all bat in the number nine spot, or even have somebody bat for 'em, right? Including the great Satchel Paige. But not Bullet Joe. No sir. He batted cleanup. That's right, cleanup. You could almost say he was like a pitching Josh Gibson."

Customer #1: "That's all good and well, but you cannot tell me that Satch can't pitch. All them pitches in his arsenal make him one tough customer on the hill. Long Tom, Midnight Rider, Bee Ball, and especially that windmill pitch."

Barber #2: "Youngblood's got a point, Ray. I'll give him that. But I'll throw out another name for you: Smokey Joe Williams. What you know about that, Ray?"

Barber #1: "Woo-wee! Smokin' Smokey Joe. I knew you would light that candle. You go hurt these boys' fragile little heads, Smitty!"

Customer #2: "Bullet Joe? Smokey Joe? Lots of Joes. Where they get they names from?"

Barber #2: "Well, that Smokey Joe, they also called him the Cyclone. And Strikeout. A whole lot of names for a whole lot of player. That man had a heater that could easily heat up the South Side in the dead of winter. That's why they called him Smokey; his fastball smoked. In an off-season game against the all-white New York Giants back in 1914, he struck out twenty players. That's right, twenty. Two-oh."

Customer #1: "Believe it or not, old-timer, but I have heard of Smokey Joe. My daddy saw him play over in Detroit years ago."

Barber #2: "I ain't surprised. He played for all kind of Negro League teams: from the San Antonio Black Broncos to the Detroit Wolves to the Brooklyn Royal Giants and a bunch more in between."

Barber #1: "That's right. He played a real long time. But what makes Smokey Joe even more special is that he carried that heater all the way through. Or I guess it carried him. Anyway, like that announcer say earlier, Smokey Joe battled that Chet Brewer at age forty-five, striking out twenty-seven Monarchs and giving up one hit. You come back to me when Satch hit that age and then we'll talk some more."

Customer #1: "Well, I don't care what you gray-hairs say. Satch is *one* of the greatest. How about we just listen to these great players in this great game on this here radio."

Barber #1: "Amen! And I think we should all tip our cap to Smitty for being a sponsor, so we could listen to this game in the first place. That little ditty they wrote for you, Smitty, was something else. You gonna have me humming it all day. 'Whether your 'do is too tall or even itty-bitty . . .' Anyway, this is the first time you boys can feel like you are there, and you have this man to thank for that. The South Side is shining today!"

Satch wasted no time in announcing his name,
earning two quick outs in the sixth frame.
Radcliffe struck out on four pitches, swinging;
then Turkey Stearnes sent a long ball singing
to Bankhead in right, who made the easy catch . . .
two outs on eight pitches, a great start for Satch.
But up next is Mule Suttles, who can certainly kick
pitches past the fence with one mighty lick.
Satch leans back, his left foot rising high;
he plants, hesitates, and then . . . his right arm lets
    fly
a blur that can't be seen by the eye,
giving the Mule strike number one
as Satch uses the windmill to get the job done,
his trademark pitch that causes frustration
for batters in the box because of that hesitation—
just short enough so batters can't time it,
just long enough so eyes can't find it.
Strike two sizzles in past Mule, letter-high,
but Satchel's next pitch punches the blue sky
as Suttles screeches a shot to shallow left,
where Vic Harris is deep but chugs in to get
closer and closer before diving quickly
to make the shoestring catch for out number three.

Top of the 7th Inning

Due Up:

Jud Wilson

Josh Gibson

Rap Dixon (replacing Vic Harris), LF (Pitt. Crawfords)

Now to the seventh inning we go,
where the West has a new pitcher in the show—
Willie Foster, the southpaw who has a stable
of pitches to pick from and bring to the table:
a sharp-breaking curve mixed with bat-burning heat
and a deceptive changeup make this veteran
　　complete.
But the crafty Foster is behind in the game
already, due to a bad start in this frame:
a single to Jud Wilson and another to Josh Gibson,
then finally, out number one from Rap Dixon,
who came on to replace the left fielder Vic
Harris of the East, with a sweet-swinging stick.

And now it's Dick Lundy at the plate and he sends
a pop fly to left field that brings in
Red Parnell, who makes the easy play,
with two men still on but now two away.
Now Chester Williams is up next to face
Foster and he singles just past first base
on the first pitch, leaving no base free,
forcing Foster to work for out number three.
The good news for the hurler is he might get a break
because Satchel's up next and an out he can make.
Satchel steps up with a difficult chore:
knock a single off Foster so his East team can score.
Foster gets started, bringing Satchel the heat,
notching strike one with a pitch that beat
Satchel's swing by a long country mile,
making Satch step out of the box and smile
because he got a taste of his own medicine,
but Satch steps back in and tunnels his vision.
Foster uncoils pitch number two,
and once again Satch swings hard through
a sinking fastball, but this time he connects
on a shot toward Radcliffe at third, who dives left
to make the out, allowing no runs
to score, and Satch and his East team are done.

A FAN IN THE STANDS

"Well, hush my mouth! That's some kind of glove you got there, Alex. That's why I voted for you. That's right. Mr. Alexander Radcliffe, current third baseman for the Chicago American Giants, I filled out my ballot in the *Chicago Defender* newspaper and checked off your name for third base. And Alex, you done me proud today, playing so hard for us fans that came to see you play. Your bat ain't been swinging too well so far, but that glove of yours is something else. I may not be able to vote for the president of my country, but I can vote for you. I'm working to change all of that, though. See, I work at the N double-A C P and we work for equal rights for Negroes. That's right, Mr. Radcliffe. They been around since 1909, but me, I only been there a couple of months, since I just graduated from Spelman College in Atlanta. But I was born and raised here in the Windy City and my daddy used to take all of us to see you play for the Giants whenever he could, and we sure had a good time. It's a real shame that everybody—Negro, white, and otherwise—can't see how good you fellas are. But with the N double-A C P, I hope to change that. That's right, Mr. Radcliffe. One of my personal goals is to get all you gentlemen playing in the big leagues by erasing that color line. I may not get to see it, but I sure hope my kids or grandkids will someday."

Renaissance Books
has the best in town;
we've got plenty to read,
so come on down.
Zora Neale Hurston,
Langston Hughes,
or W. E. B. DuBois
are just a few you can choose.
We've been here
on the South Side for ages,

so come and let your fingers
flip through our pages.
Knowledge is power
and books are the key,
and Renaissance has plenty
to set your mind free.

Bottom of the 7th Inning
Due Up:
Red Parnell
Sam Bankhead
Larry Brown, C (Chi. Amer. Giants)

Folks, here we go, back to the game,
where Satch has racked up two outs in this frame;
Parnell hit to second for out number one,
and Bankhead popped out number two to Gibson.
Satchel has shown great efficiency
in earning two outs, but now needs strike three
on Brown, who stands with a count of two
balls and strikes as Satch lifts his left shoe
up to the sky; he plants, and then
his right arm rears back, whipping a wind
that blows by Brown like a hurricane breeze—
STRIKE THREE down the pipe, just above the knees.
Out number three, a thing of beauty
as Satchel continues his mound artistry.

Top of the 8th Inning

Due Up:

Cool Papa Bell

Cy Perkins (batting in Jimmie Crutchfield's spot),
   C (Pitt. Crawfords)

Oscar Charleston

The Eastern bats have picked up the pace
as Cool Papa Bell stands on first base,
due to a walk given up by Willie
Foster on the hill, which could possibly
be just the break this East team needs,
because Bell will try to use his speed
to get to second base and more,
and do whatever he can to score.
A change in the lineup at spot number two
will bring up Cy Perkins, a great player who
will catch for Gibson and replace Crutchfield

in the lineup, and Gibson will head to right field
because there is no way Gibson leaves this game;
there are too many fans here chanting his name.
No, Dick Lundy will give Josh a rest
from his backstop duties to pressure the West.
Back to the rubber, where Foster stands
with two strikes on Perkins from the skill of his hand.
He looks to first base, where Cool Papa awaits,
faces Perkins, winds up . . . and Bell briskly breaks
into a sprint, attempting to steal
second base, and he . . . closes the deal!
Brown, the catcher, made a good throw,
but Cool Papa, folks, can make lightning look slow,
and that's what he did with cat-quick ease,
but at least Foster got strike number three,
sitting down Perkins for out number one,
though Bell has a look that says he's not done.

A FAN IN THE STANDS
Section 132, Lower Deck,
directly behind home plate
"Go, Cool Papa B., go! Cool Papa. That's a
funny name. Why they call you that? I heard
they call you the Tan Cheetah too. My daddy

talk about you all the time. He say you the fastest man in the Negro Leagues and can't nobody catch you. My daddy say you so fast that you could turn the lights out and be in bed before it gets dark. That's fast. I don't know if I believe all of that, but he also said that one time in a game you scored on a bunt. I didn't know what a bunt was, but he explained it to me and if you did that, that's real fast. My daddy also say one time you hit the ball right up the middle and you ran so fast that you got hit by your own ball and they called you out. That's too fast. I don't know if I believe all of that, either. My daddy say that Jesse Owens is scared to race you on account of how fast your feet are. I wanna see that because everybody know how fast Jesse is. My daddy say that you have stolen the most bases in the Negro Leagues, so what I wanna know, Cool Papa, is, if you stole all those bases, when you gonna give 'em back?"

One on, two out as Foster faces Wilson,
standing in the box, hoping to knock in
Bell with a single or even a double,
but Wilson has gotten himself into trouble
by swinging early, earning two strikes,
then his next swing connects, sending Bell's spikes
shooting toward third as the ball rolls through
second and short as Bell races to
home plate in a hurry with the speed of a gazelle . . .
and slides in to score, does Cool Papa Bell!
The Tan Cheetah's feet sure did fly
from second to home in the blink of an eye.
Top of the eighth with two outs still gone,
Foster versus Gibson, who will look to go long.
Foster rears back and releases . . . STRIKE ONE!
A fast curve that broke as Josh mightily swung,
but he missed as that ball hissed
with snap and pop from Foster's fingertips.
Gibson steps out to kick at his cleats
as a cascade of sound pours down from the seats.
Josh steps back in, his cleats scratching the box,
as Willie whistles in a fastball Josh knocks
deep . . . deep . . . deep into right;
that ball has got wings and just might take flight.
Bankhead goes back, back toward the wall,

then leaps from his feet . . . and snatches the ball
out of the air—OH MY! OH MY!
That smack from Gibson PUNCTURED the sky
for a brief moment, but here in Chicago
the wind can play tricks when it decides to blow
this way or that, and Josh Gibson's bat
missed a four-bagger by a quick finger snap.
And for the second time today
Gibson was robbed on another great play.
Don't go anywhere, because we aren't done;
the West is up next, now down by one run.

Bottom of the 8th Inning

Due Up:
**Andy Patterson (replacing Sammy Hughes
    at 2nd), 2B (Cleveland Red Sox)**
Willie Foster, P (Chi. Amer. Giants)
Willie Wells

Sammy Hughes gets replaced by Andy Patterson,
but he went down swinging for out number one.
Foster, the pitcher, is now clutching a bat
and he bloops a single where no one is at,

just over the head of Lundy, the shortstop;
who knew that Foster's bat had pop?
And that is the first single off Satch,
as Lundy leaped high but couldn't quite catch
the single by Willie, and now the West
can put the great Satchel Paige to the test.
The East team, folks, can feel the heat
as Willie "the Devil" Wells leaves his seat
and approaches the box, looking to swing
a shot off Satchel and possibly bring
Foster from first to score his team a run,
but Satchel has other ideas . . . STRIKE ONE!
Whoa, folks, that pitch is making ME choke
because that ball left a gray trail of smoke.
Wells stood like a statue as the pitch came in,
and the next pitch from Satch . . . burns the Devil
      again,
zipping right past Willie's swing with the gas,
bringing strike two as Satchel works fast.
Willie steps out to slow the pace down
while Satchel pops gum from high on the mound.
Willie steps back in and Satchel begins
his windup and whips a pitch laced with spin
that rotates toward Willie deceptively quick,
then drops at the plate from twelve o'clock to six,

diving directly beneath Wells's swinging bat—
strike three on the Devil came just like that.
Two outs, one on, with the West still behind
by one lone run, but they need to find
a way to get a run on the board,
and that task falls to Radcliffe, no easy chore.
Alex Radcliffe, the third baseman, has made
some great plays with his glove, but his bat has
    stayed
silent as he has gone 0 for 3;
his team needs a hit from him desperately.
The first pitch arrives and he takes a huge cut,
ending the rally by popping the ball up
to Dixon in left, who camps out under it,
then snares the dropping pop fly in his mitt.
Satch has been masterful since he came in,
and if he continues, his East team will win.

Top of the 9th Inning
Due Up:
Rap Dixon
Dick Lundy
Chester Williams

The East is at bat and they have a hit
from Rap Dixon, who singled past Mule Suttles's
    mitt.
A potential run, but out number one
came next when Dick Lundy hit to Patterson
the fielder at second, and that's where we stand,
one on, one out, and Chester Williams, the man
standing in the box with a count of
two balls and one strike, as the pitch smacks the
    glove
of Brown, the catcher, who jumps up to deal
a hard throw to second, while Dixon tries to steal
the base but is easily tagged

because Patterson snags
the great throw from Brown and manages to bag
out number two on the East, but that
still leaves Williams holding the bat
in the box with a count of two and two
because that last pitch came in straight and true
to serve up a strike, but now Foster sends
a changeup to Williams as he swings on and bends
past second base into shallow left field,
putting Williams on base, and folks, he has a feel
for the bat today because now he has three
hits in this game from swinging so free.
Through three innings Foster has pitched up and
    down,
throwing strikeouts and giving up hits from the
    mound,
but now he's ahead, facing Satch in the box,
tossing two quick strikes and one ball toward his
    socks.
Now Willie begins his windup and proceeds
to catch Satchel off guard, buckling his knees
with a changeup that ambles to the plate slow,
using the same motion he uses to throw
that blistering fastball, deceiving the pace
to sit Satch down and strand Williams on base,

because due to strike three, that made OUT three
and ended the East team's chance of a rally.

Lace up your dance shoes
and come do your thing
on the South Side at
Sadie's House of Swing.
Put some pep in your step
and some glide in your stride;
let the rhythm of the music
take your feet on a ride.
We've got bands
and dancing, too,

that will shake and stomp the blues
right out of you.
If Ellington and Basie
make you crazy and sing,
then come to the South Side
to Sadie's House of Swing.
The Count Basie Orchestra will swing back
into town September 3rd through the 12th, so
forget the blues
and bring your dancing shoes!

Bottom of the 9th Inning
Due Up:
Turkey Stearnes
Mule Suttles
Red Parnell

Bottom of the ninth is now where we start,
with Satch on the hill facing the heart
of the West lineup, who will now try
to score at least one run and tie
this game, but they blew their first shot
as Turkey came up to bat and got
struck out by Satch, who is pitching to perfection,
mixing up speed with precision and deception.
But coming up next to swing the big stick
is Mule Suttles as fans chant, "Kick, Mule, kick!"
These fans want to see more action happen
today so they can continue their cheering and
    clapping
for these sepia stars shining today,
who've given their all on each and every play.
Big Mule steps in and the chant continues
to grow louder as Satch flips in ball two,
making the count two balls and one
strike on the Mule, who sure has had fun

in this star-studded battle at age thirty-three,
playing the game with youthful energy.
Suttles settles into his bat stance
as Satchel submits a curveball that lands
square on the sweet spot of Mule's bat, and he
kicks the ball HARD to right with fury.
Josh Gibson gives chase, but this ball will land
just out of reach of the right fielder's hand.
As Suttles nears second, Gibson rears back
and strong-arms a throw to stop Mule in his tracks,
holding him to second in what could have been
a stand-up triple if not for Gibson.
Suttles comes through with a big clutch hit,
showing these fans the Mule can still kick.

A FAN IN THE STANDS
SECTION 138, LOWER DECK RESERVED,
THIRD BASE SIDE OVER DUGOUT

"Kick, Mule, kick! Fine piece of hitting right there, Mule. I see you still swinging a mean stick. Always could. I remember when we was both playing for the Black Barons in Birmingham some years ago and watchin' you wallop that ball out the park every single day. I heard some fellas here earlier saying Josh Gibson was the best slugger in the league, and I just had to put my two cents in and let 'em know about the Mule. The man that kicks balls out the park and introduces them to the moon with one mighty swing. I told them fellas about the one time we was playing in the Cuban Winter League and you put a real hurt on the ball and sent it clear over the 500-foot mark in center field with plenty of room to spare. I swear that ball kissed the clouds and drew rain, you hit it so high. And that bat of yours! A big ole 50-ounce chunk of lumber that nobody could swing but you. And boy, did you swing it. I see you can still swing it with the best of 'em, so keep on kicking, Mule. Because as long as the Mule is kicking, I'll be watching."

Satchel is close to out number two
on Red Parnell, who scratches each shoe
in the box with one ball and two strikes;
the next pitch from Satch is one Parnell likes
as he swings and shoots a ground ball to Chester
Williams at second, who flashes the leather
by making the catch with a backhanded grab
to his right, then turns to make the tag
on Suttles off base, but Williams isn't done—
he spins and throws to first, and Charleston
stretches to beat Parnell on the run.
A great double play for outs two and three
from Williams, who made it look so easy,
ends the inning and ends the game,
meaning today the East will be named
champions of this East-West Classic
in a game that was indeed a classic.
One run to none, the East finally scored
in the eighth inning, and folks, what more
could you possibly ask for?
We had Josh Gibson swinging harder than Count
   Basie
but robbed twice in almost the same way exactly.
We had Willie Wells showing off his skill
at shortstop, and we had Jimmie Crutchfield

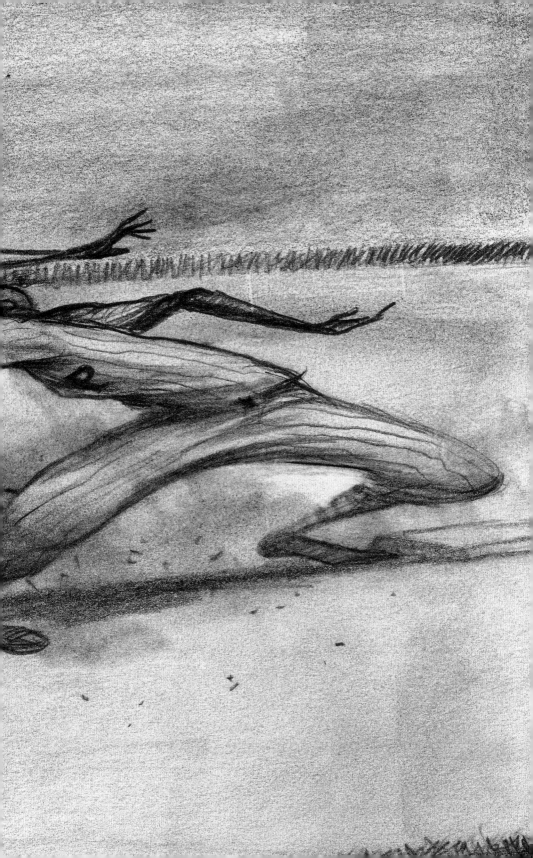

make a dandy of a throw for a fine double play,
just one of three turned in today.
We had Turkey and Mule in this pitchers' duel
flash leather and kick, and we had Cool
Papa Bell score the winning run with ease
and show why he's one of the league's best thieves.
We had heaters and hurricanes whipped from the
    hands
of pitchers with names like Slim and Tin Can.
We had strikeouts and hits and many a great catch,
but in the end, folks, it came down to Satch
showing his skill on the high hill,
baffling batters with the round white pill,
racking up outs and many a K;
Satch and all these men came to play.
The fans are now showing their appreciation
by saluting these men with a standing ovation.

"Thank you, Oscar Charleston."
"Thank you, Josh Gibson."
"Thank you, Willie Wells."
"Thank you, Jimmie Crutchfield."
"Thank you, Turkey Stearnes."
"Thank you, Satchel Paige."
"Thank you, Alex Radcliffe."

"Thank you, Cool Papa Bell."
"Thank you, Mule Suttles."

To *all* Negro League players, I say "thanks"
    personally—
thank you for creating everlasting memories.
To all our sponsors and listeners here in the Windy
    City,
this is Lester Roberts signing off on WNLB.

Author's Note

The beauty of sport is that two teams can meet on the field of play to determine who's best. But what happens when athletes aren't allowed to compete against each other because of the color of their skin? Can the winner truly claim to be the best if everyone isn't allowed to compete?

This was the question black baseball players faced as they embraced America's pastime in an era when the professional game didn't embrace them. So they created their own baseball league, which became known as the Negro League. Star players soon emerged and were often compared to top major league players of the day.

When Major League Baseball chose to have an all-star game to celebrate their best, the Negro League thought it would be a great way to showcase the stars in their league and decided to do the same. They called it the East-West Classic and held it in Chicago.

I chose to focus on the second all-star game because in the first game, the teams were made up of two regular teams with a few additional players split onto each side. The result was a high-scoring game that left many fans voicing their complaints at not being able to see their favorite players.

The owners heard the fans loud and clear, so the following year the fans were allowed to vote in their favorite players, and a true East-West Classic was born.

Once word got around that the best Negro League ball-players would be on display in Chicago, the Classic was THE place to see and be seen. But as good as the Negro League players were, and as much as the fans loved them, for years they were denied the opportunity to compete against their white counterparts to determine who was truly the best. And in the end, isn't that what sports are all about?